Earthsigns

Haiku North America Anthologies

Harvest (1991)

The Shortest Distance (1993)

Northern Lights (1995)

Shades of Green (1997)

Too Busy for Spring (1999)

Paperclips (2001)

Brocade of Leaves (2003)

Tracing the Fern (2005)

Dandelion Wind (2007)

Into Our Words (2009)

Standing Still (2011)

Close to the Wind (2013)

Fire in the Treetops (2015)

Earthsigns (2017)

Earthsigns

*An anthology of poems commemorating
the 2017 Haiku North America conference*

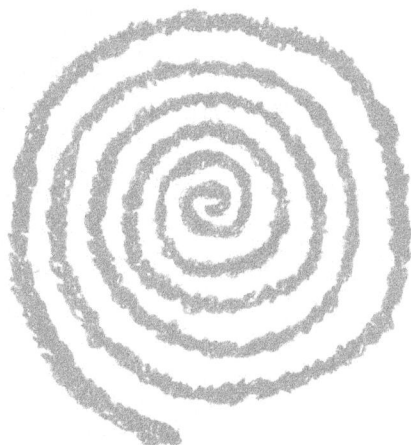

Michael Dylan Welch
and Scott Wiggerman, *Editors*

Lidia Rozmus, *Illustrations*

PRESS HERE
Sammamish, Washington

PRESS HERE
22230 NE 28th Place
Sammamish, Washington
98074-6408 USA

ISBN 978-1-878798-38-1

First printing, September 2017

This book is a commemorative anthology of poems by attendees
and participants in Haiku North America 2017, an international
celebration of haiku and related genres of poetry held in
Santa Fe, New Mexico, from September 13 through 17, 2017.
Each attendee who chose to submit poems was guaranteed
to have one selected for inclusion in this anthology.

Design, typography, and art direction by Michael Dylan Welch.
Poems and names set in 16/20 Chaparral Pro and 12/16 Myriad Pro Italic,
with headings set in 26/28 Rockwell Condensed.

www.haikunorthamerica.com

Your World for the Moment

Renowned Santa Fe artist Georgia O'Keeffe said, "When you take a flower in your hand and really look at it, it's your world for the moment. I want to give that world to someone else." We find such sharing and celebration in this book's poems. *Earthsigns* collects haiku and senryu by 183 attendees of the 2017 Haiku North America conference. Each poem is your world for the moment, a flower of sorts, a sign of the earth.

Haiku celebrate personal surroundings and experiences as they unfold through the seasons. This collection focuses mostly on Southwest images—not only from participants who live in the region but also from many who have visited. With petroglyph-inspired images by Lidia Rozmus, this anthology offers a strong sense of the 2017 conference, its speakers and attendees, and its location, Santa Fe, in the heart of New Mexico.

Haiku North America began in 1991 and has moved around the continent every two years since then. With the 2017 gathering, HNA comes to the American Southwest for the first time, attracting its largest attendance in the event's history and consequently its largest conference anthology, *Earthsigns*. Here you can read poems by many of the leading haiku poets writing in English today, along with what may be the first published haiku by new conference attendees. In all, these poems are signs of an enthusiastic, welcoming, and vigorous community.

This fourteenth anthology in HNA's history follows previous collections in arranging poems by each poet's first name, with the aspiration that we remain on a first-name basis, as friends with each other and friends in the haiku art. May each poem be a flower in your hand, your world for the moment.

Michael Dylan Welch
Scott Wiggerman

crickets
perforate the night . . .
constellations

Agnes Eva Savich
Austin, Texas

wearing a blue
I have never seen before
Sangre de Cristos

Alan S. Bridges
Littleton, Massachusetts

what I thought
was wilderness
potsherds

Alanna C. Burke
Santa Fe, New Mexico

A dinner bell empties the baseball field

Alexis Rotella
Arnold, Maryland

spotting
the bristlecone pines
—autumn drizzle

Alison Woolpert
Santa Cruz, California

canyon sunset . . .
so much of his story
I never knew

Angela Terry
Lake Forest Park, Washington

desert noon—
even the organ pipes
fall silent

Anita Curran Guenin
San Diego, California

rain before dawn
a prayer
for my daughter

Arlie Parker
Laguna Niguel, California

dentalium regalia
from deep in the ocean
a story of belonging

Astrid Egger
Queen Charlotte, British Columbia

after silence
a monk
wakes up
the bell

Ava Dasya Rasa
Santa Fe, New Mexico

雷雨きて揺れる葉むらの小鳥たち
raiu kite yureru hamura no kotoritachi

thunderstorm—
the shapes of birds
among the swaying leaves

Aya Yuhki
Tokyo, Japan

June bug—
a circuitous route
to enlightenment

Barbara Hay
Tulsa, Oklahoma

fallen oak leaves
on the porch
empty shoes

Basia Miller
Santa Fe, New Mexico

night of stars—
old wooden crosses lean
into the land

Betty Arnold
Saratoga, California

saltgrass
quick to reveal
old hurts

Beverly Acuff Momoi
Mountain View, California

rubbing oil
into the baseball glove
birthday snow

Bill Cooper
Midlothian, Virginia

beginner
praying the seed
into the earth

Bill Kenney
Whitestone, New York

turquoise and silver
sunrise washing
over Santa Fe

Bill Pauly
Asbury, Iowa

pink hoodoos
only my left arm
sunburned

Billie Dee
Las Cruces, New Mexico

right on the tip of my tongue mother's voice

Bob Moyer
Winston Salem, North Carolina

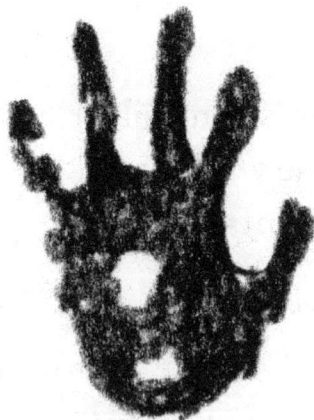

lightning flash
streaking
abstract art

Bona M. Santos
Los Angeles, California

white hiking socks
a little less
Red Rock country

*Brad Bennett
Arlington, Massachusetts*

cat in my suitcase
on neatly folded clothes
imminent loneliness

*Brian DeMuth
Bowie, Maryland*

pops of yellow
punctuate a forest walk—
birdsong

Carol Judkins
Carlsbad, California

wildflowers
among the debris
. . . tent city

Carole MacRury
Point Roberts, Washington

deadheading blossoms
still no news
about the bank loan

Caroline Giles Banks
Minneapolis, Minnesota

a plum branch
drops petals to my desk . . .
the finished painting

Carolyn Fitz
Scotts Valley, California

acorn rain
the part of my brain
that knew how to spell

Carolyn Hall
San Francisco, California

new table
the years it took
to grow the trees

Carolyn Winkler
Portland, Oregon

walking uphill
labored breath carried away
on an easy breeze

Catherine Gardner
Arch Cape, Oregon

sea breeze
    the salt taste
in her kiss

Ce Rosenow
Eugene, Oregon

filling the night
with forest
new moon

Chandra Bales
Albuquerque, New Mexico

waking from a dream
without a center
misty crescent moon

Charles Trumbull
Santa Fe, New Mexico

stone walls
echoing
the river's refrain

Cheryl Berrong
Fairbanks, Alaska

garden pond—
a lizard's blue belly
floats among clouds

Christine Horner
Lafayette, California

gilded flower moon
wedding in Mexico
luna de miel

Christine Wenk-Harrison
Lago Vista, Texas

ribbon chert
the deeper
its layers

Chuck Brickley
Daly City, California

ancient hearth sunspot on the floor of a pueblo

Claudia Coutu Radmore
Carleton Place, Ontario

en mar azul
como ballenas muertas
dos rocas negras

on the blue sea
like dead whales
two black rocks

Cristina Rascón
Ciudad de México, México

slave quarters
in one brick
a thumbprint

Crystal Simone Smith
Durham, North Carolina

My view clearer
with every
falling leaf

Cydney Brown
Basalt, Colorado

giant sequoia
how long before the child
doesn't need my hand

Cyndi Lloyd
Riverton, Utah

tumbleweeds
between the tombstones
cold desert wind

Cynthia Kowalski Henderson
Santa Fe, New Mexico

tap tap of branches
against my window glass
snap snap of far-off wings

Dale Harris
Albuquerque, New Mexico

unable to rest
on the earth
horsetail clouds

Dan Schwerin
Greendale, Wisconsin

sky in the footprints I muddled through

Dave Russo
Cary, North Carolina

Rain on my window
gently running down in streams
Strontium 90

Dave Siegel
Cincinnati, Ohio

zen garden
someone's blue gum
in the waves

David G. Lanoue
New Orleans, Louisiana

shorter days
the leaves and my hair
change color

David Oates
Athens, Georgia

peak colors
in the cauliflower
a pearl of dew

Deb Koen
Rochester, New York

years
measured in rock . . .
that same old question

Deborah P Kolodji
Temple City, California

a lone iris with the lilies what to do

Denise Fontaine-Pincince
Belchertown, Massachusetts

rocking lightly
in a slight breeze
cicada shell

Don Wentworth
Pittsburgh, Pennsylvania

cardinal whistles
wake up
get up
sun's up

Doris Ann Hayes
Burlington, Wisconsin

finally sky resembles earth Ghost Ranch sunset

Doris Lynch
Bloomington, Indiana

leaning on the fence
the full moon and I
share secrets

Eileen Benavente-Blas
Dededo, Guam

mango-colored house
startling neighbors at first sight
over time delights

Elaine Parker Adams
Houston, Texas

poppies bedeck hills
golden at sunrise
Easter morning

Elizabeth Yahn Williams
San Luis Rey, California

cold stars
light the snowdrifts . . .
sparks from the snowplow

Ellen Ryan
Lone Tree, Colorado

one soft feather
found in the gutter
my favorite alley

Erin Castaldi
Mays Landing, New Jersey

global warming . . .
a stamp from Mars
on the envelope

Fay Aoyagi
San Francisco, California

terracotta moon
the door propped open
with a broom

Francine Banwarth
Dubuque, Iowa

Moving . . .
I take my seashell collection
back to the beach

Garry Gay
Santa Rosa, California

dark enough
our grandson wonders
what stars do

Gary Hotham
Scaggsville, Maryland

war of attrition
tierra amarilla
surrounds the mesa

Gary Vaughn
Albuquerque, New Mexico

cars upended in a farmer's field
horns blare into black soil

Gayle Lauradunn
Albuquerque, New Mexico

slipping into
the red soil
deer skull

Gregory Longenecker
Pasadena, California

the way the stones
of the old wall lean . . .
I take your hand

Hannah Mahoney
Cambridge, Massachusetts

between
cat and carp
the dappled light

Henry Brann
Philadelphia, Pennsylvania

fading daylight
the empty swing
still swinging

Jacquie Pearce
Vancouver, British Columbia

sun drops behind towers
my shadow
on stilts

Jane Munro
Vancouver, British Columbia

autumn beneath sycamores
fallen stars litter the ground

Janet Ruth
Corrales, New Mexico

wind and light
play with the clouds
where Georgia called home

Janis Albright Lukstein
Rancho Palos Verdes, California

at dusk
the quail's call remaps
the shifting dunes

Jari Thymian
Sioux Falls, South Dakota

two birds merge
into one
reflection

Jean Ann Hunt
Plattsburgh, New York

our deep talk drowned out crashing waves

Jeannie Martin
Arlington, Massachusetts

dust bathing
a jackrabbit
kind of day

Jeff Hoagland
Hopewell, New Jersey

morning coffee
the roses and i
find some common ground

Jennifer Hambrick
Columbus, Ohio

before my time
a thunder egg
split in two

Jennifer Sutherland
Viewbank, Australia

day's end
two kids hand in hand
skipping shadows

Jerome Cushman
Victor, New York

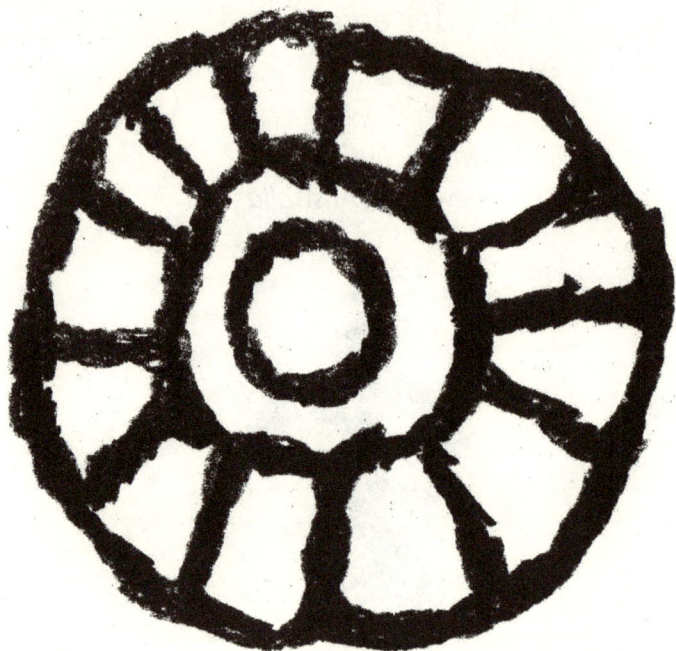

after the fight
we bury
the campfire

Jessica Tremblay
Burnaby, British Columbia

beach glass
the blue
of its wave

Jill Lange
Cleveland Heights, Ohio

sacred mountain
tribal towns
all around

Jim Applegate
Roswell, New Mexico

through a cold mist
yellow
where spring is

Jim Kacian
Winchester, Virginia

sharing spicy tamales
our conversation
perks up

Joan Prefontaine
Cottonwood, Arizona

Indian casino
the roulette ball lands
on green

Joe McKeon
Strongsville, Ohio

Sonoran Desert
saguaro's arms
embrace the sun

John J. Candelaria
Corrales, New Mexico

a little blood ownership of land

John Stevenson
Nassau, New York

summer twilight
a beer bottle flickers
in the weeds

John Zheng
Itta Bena, Mississippi

penny for your thoughts
he says . . . she says
way too much

Johnye Strickland
Maumelle, Arkansas

Down in the canyon
the yellow light of a hogan—
threat of male rain

Josette Pellet
Lausanne, Switzerland

beneath the night sky
I mindlessly savor
burgundy moonshine

Judy K. Mosher
Santa Fe, New Mexico

white yucca flowers
irreversible time
at Trinity

Jules Nyquist
Albuquerque, New Mexico

the shape of her hands the shape of the bowl the

Julie Warther
Dover, Ohio

firefly!
    hitching a ride
on its own light

Kala Ramesh
Pune, India

guitar solo
 reminds us of
  what words can't

Karen Sohne
Toronto, Ontario

scent of earth
a towhee in and out
of the sage

Karina M. Young
Salinas, California

canyon and mesa
how the landscape of my life
begins to match

Kath Abela Wilson
Pasadena, California

drought over rain colors the river

Kathe L. Palka
Flemington, New Jersey

winter moon
snowy owls hunting
in my dreams

Kathleen O'Toole
Takoma Park, Maryland

a sign of rain
the smell of earth
in distant thunder

Katsuhiko Momoi
Mountain View, California

Normandy church chimes
our bateau glides past
gold-brown corn fields

Kay Tashner
Bronxville, New York

snow
on the blue hills
day moon

kjmunro
Whitehorse, Yukon Territory

blossom petals
in the old diary . . .
earth tones

kris moon (kondo)
Kiyokawa, Japan

fall memorial—
your business card remains
in my shirt pocket

Lenard D. Moore
Raleigh, North Carolina

too late braking the hitchhiker's middle finger

Lew Watts
Santa Fe, New Mexico

Ghost Ranch
no need
for a dreamcatcher

Lidia Rozmus
Vernon Hills, Illinois

flyover country—
the speck of a tractor
plowing dusk

Linda Papanicolaou
Palo Alto, California

vintage ring its life before us

Linda Weir
Bowie, Maryland

trickster wind
a beach ball
travels down the coast

Lynne Jambor
Vancouver, British Columbia

moon rising
as gentle as
touching snow

Makoto Nakanishi
Matsuyama, Japan

rain in the fields
white-naped cranes
bend their necks

Marcyn Del Clements
Claremont, California

out of pockmarked cliffs
the jagged flight
of swallows

Margaret Chula
Portland, Oregon

alive as it's ever been
earthworm in the robin's bill

Marian Olson
Santa Fe, New Mexico

worn smooth by wind
layers of light seep
into a cavern

Marietta McGregor
Canberra, Australia

walking the wash
hints of distant thunder
in the glint of mica

Marilyn Ashbaugh
Edwardsburg, Michigan

where I lived as a child
why don't I remember
that large dead tree?

Marilyn Shoemaker Hazelton
Allentown, Pennsylvania

in the waterless canyon driftwood logjam

Marshall B. Hatch III
Deerfield, New Hampshire

even the shadows dazzle

moss-strewn mounds

under budding maples

Marshall Hryciuk
Toronto, Ontario

blood-streaked statue
in a dusty brown land
jarring my faith

Mary Heron
Elkins Park, Pennsylvania

Spring mountain water
Funneled to an ancient pool
Crystalline mirror

Mary Jane Corwin
Massillon, Ohio

the sky folds
encircles our black earth
another bomb

Mary Kite
Santa Fe, New Mexico

geranium leaves
turn towards the sound of chimes
rain fills the space

Mary Sherman
Pecos, New Mexico

waxed apples
am told I have
my mother's smile

Maxianne Berger
Montréal, Québec

roadrunner
dashes across the road
always last minute

Maya Lazarus
Caldwell, Texas

hill and half-moon
growing brighter as they grow apart

Melissa J White
Santa Fe, New Mexico

bony windmills
slice the air
driving to your funeral

Meta L. Schettler
Fresno, California

woods walk—
I catch the cobwebs
that miss my son

Michael Dylan Welch
Sammamish, Washington

holding the sunset
the red clay
of the infield

Michael Ketchek
Rochester, New York

late summer dusk
a crimson tinge
to the underwing

Michele Root-Bernstein
East Lansing, Michigan

this burnt wooden spoon
she used . . .
blackberry jam

Mimi Ahern
San Jose, California

I felt I should leave out part of what
I told you—sandstone arch

Miriam Sagan
Santa Fe, New Mexico

Old cowboy boots
Lined up on shelves, side by side
Waiting to two-step

Nancy Beauregard
Santa Fe, New Mexico

Earth Day—
the pungent smell of
lemongrass soup

Patricia J. Machmiller
San Jose, California

Tall slender grasses
Courtyard dancers
Inviting me in

Patricia Pearce
Santa Fe, New Mexico

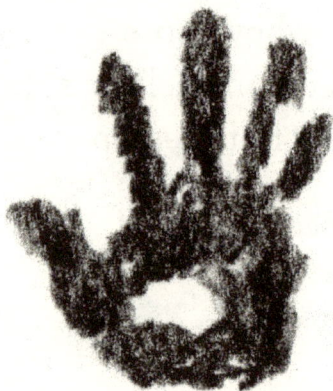

this monster moon
washing away starlight
where has it been

Patsy Kate Booth
Pueblo, Colorado

telling time from the clock
only my father knew
how to wind

Patti Niehoff
Cincinnati, Ohio

deleting her
last text
scent of snow

paul m.
Bristol, Rhode Island

firehouse fish fry—
from the makeshift stage
the banjo's heat

Penny Harter
Mays Landing, New Jersey

dirt, sand, metal
ash, metal
back from Iraq

Phyllis Culham
Annapolis, Maryland

even the hummingbird
disappointed
with my petunias

Rich Schnell
Port Douglas, New York

the weight of privilege passing clouds

Rick Tarquinio
Woodruff, New Jersey

stars in the night sky
meanwhile in my dark office
glowing LEDs

Rick Wilson
Pasadena, California

winterberry among fifty shades of brown

Robert Ertman
Annapolis, Maryland

heavy august day
crows circling
just circling

Robert Forsythe
Annandale, Virginia

the park road
   would take longer . . .
      month of leaves

Robert Gilliland
Austin, Texas

lavacados
a bowl of rockamole
a salad o' puns

Robert Thomas Lundy
Del Mar, California

Global warming:
January
with fruit flies

Robin Palley
Philadelphia, Pennsylvania

my inner Chiyo-ni
walking the red path
to Chimayó

Robin White
Deerfield, New Hampshire

on the dune fence
looking out to sea
a pair of lost glasses

Rocky Wilson
Camden, New Jersey

desert wind—
his city veneer
erodes

Ruth Powell
Prince George, British Columbia

warm brown rocks
after our skinny dip
feeling the curves

Ruth Yarrow
Ithaca, New York

mammatus clouds
the cries of hawks
build above me

Sandi Pray
St. Johns, Florida

leaves
    raked into a pile
        second divorce

Scott Glander
Glenview, Illinois

Chaco Canyon
the cottonwood wind
sotto voce

Scott Mason
Chappaqua, New York

mountain's outline
the difference walking
alone

Scott Wiggerman
Albuquerque, New Mexico

sparkle of sunshine
set to music—
meandering stream

Sharon K. Young
Tok, Alaska

cliff boxes and ladders
in an abandoned Navajo dwelling
desert earth

Sharon Lynne Yee
Torrance, California

tule elk . . .
recalculating
the way home

Sharon Pretti
San Francisco, California

wild ponies
behind barbed wire
gathering clouds

Sharon Rhutasel-Jones
Los Ranchos, New Mexico

ochre, umber, sienna
tones on the scale
of rock hardness

Sheila Sondik
Bellingham, Washington

wisteria curtains—
inviting bees
pushing us out

Shinko Fushimi
Mito, Japan

earthtones
measuring the truth
of water

Sondra J. Byrnes
Santa Fe, New Mexico

on the porch
moonlit dust
untouched

Sonia Coman-Ernstoff
New York, New York

dancing above
the lime-green pond . . .
red dragonflies

Steve Sharp
Maumelle, Arkansas

shelves of dusty shoes
the cobbler tapping
a jazzy beat

Steve Tabb
Boise, Idaho

the day long amidst redwoods myriad faiths

Susan Diridoni
Kensington, California

grazing at dawn
throngs of sandhill cranes
almost silent

Susan Smith
Austin, Texas

above tree line
our differences fade

Tami Fraser
Basalt, Colorado

hummingbird—
talk of building
a wall

Tanya McDonald
Woodinville, Washington

summer heat
the tomato
slips its skin

Terri L. French
Huntsville, Alabama

東北に春あちこちとふきのとう
tōhoku ni haru achikochi to fukinotō

Tōhoku's spring—
here and there
the butterbur buds

Teruko Kumei
Tokyo, Japan

Wind kisses the moon—
laughter lofts boys
dangling in a tree

Tiffany Austin
Nassau, Bahamas

alluvium
I pocket a stone
meant for the sea

Tom Painting
Atlanta, Georgia

two hidden doves
in a pine tree at sunset . . .
summer song

Tyrone A. Wright
Santa Fe, New Mexico

Similkameen
the river rolls
off my tongue

Vicki McCullough
Vancouver, British Columbia

serious november
the lean of a snow fence
toward the hard brown field

Wanda D. Cook
Hadley, Massachusetts

vineyard casita . . .
do the wind chimes
ever rest?

William Scott Galasso
Laguna Woods, California

such a drowsy fragrance
wafting through the third-floor window—
violas

Yoko's Dogs
(Jan Conn, Mary di Michele, Susan Gillis, Jane Munro)

summer rays
my story
evaporates

Yvette Nicole Kolodji
Encino, California

train window
I reflect
into the woods

Zoanne Schnell
Keeseville, New York

Contributors

www.ingramcontent.com/pod-product-compliance
Lightning Source LLC
La Vergne TN
LVHW041307080426
835510LV00009B/890